SIGNS THAT YOU MIGHT BE UNDER CRIMINAL INVESTIGATION

SIGNS THAT YOU MIGHT BE UNDER CRIMINAL INVESTIGATION

JAMES P WHALEN

Whalen Law Office

ISBN: 1515202747
ISBN 13: 9781515202745
Library of Congress Control Number: 2015912084
CreateSpace Independent Publishing Platform
North Charleston, South Carolina

INTRODUCTION

THE PURPOSE OF this book is to help the typical person identify if they are under a federal criminal investigation for a white collar crime and how to take the appropriate steps. The first question the book will answer is, "How will I know if I am under investigation for a white collar crime?" There are generally four tell-tale signs that you may be the subject of a criminal investigation, which I will help you to recognize. The second question this book will answer is, "I recognize these four signs...now what do I do?" There are five things you should do when you are in this situation, which will be explained on the upcoming pages. Failing to heed this advice could hinder your ability to defend yourself against the massive federal government!

The advice in this book comes from over 19 years of experience working with several of these agencies including the Small Business Administration; Department of Education, Health and Human Services; and the Federal Housing and Finance Administration as well as the Department of Justice and the United States Attorney's office.

PART ONE
HOW WILL I KNOW?

1

CONTACTED BY A FEDERAL OR STATE
LAW ENFORCEMENT AGENT

I N MANY CASES, a federal law enforcement agent will contact people who they suspect may be involved in a crime well before they actually charge someone with a crime.

There are numerous federal agencies that investigate criminal activity. The common ones are listed below:

- Federal Bureau of Investigation (FBI)
- Alcohol, Tobacco, Firearms and Explosives (ATFE)
- Drug Enforcement Administration (DEA)
- Internal Revenue Service-Criminal Investigations Division (IRS)
- Immigration and Customs Enforcement (ICE)
- U.S. Customs and Border Protection (CBP)
- U.S. Secret Service
- U.S. Marshal Service
- U.S. Postal Inspection Service
- Fish and Wildlife Service

Additionally, most if not all, federal agencies have an Office of Inspector General, or **OIG**, which employ agents to investigate crimes, make arrests and bring charges against individuals.

Most federal law enforcement agents do not wear any type of uniform and work in what is called "plain clothes." This is usually business attire, such as a suit and tie. They also generally travel in teams of two. If they suspect you are part of an organization that may be under investigation, they may contact you by coming to your home, place of employment, or by calling you. These agents may try to talk to you about the company for which you work, manage, or own, and perhaps even about other employees of the company.

It is not always a federal law enforcement agency that will be contacting you during the initial stages of an investigation. Sometimes state law enforcement agencies will be involved as well. If you are contacted by any government or law enforcement agency, it is safe to assume that you may be under investigation.

While it may not seem like you are the target of their visit, it is still very important to discuss the event with an experienced criminal defense attorney before speaking with any law enforcement agent.

2

Subpoena for Business Documents

I F A FEDERAL prosecutor's office, known as the United States Attorney's office, has filed a grand jury subpoena for any type of business documents, it is a clear sign that you or someone connected to you may be under investigation. Most federal white collar crimes involve business transactions that are documented on paper. Therefore, these types of investigations begin with the collection and review of those documents. The investigations can involve mortgage loans, bank loans, stock purchases, oil and gas investments, and Medicare/Medicaid billing, just to name a few. The subpoena is usually a grand jury subpoena served by a federal law enforcement agent or an Assistant United States Attorney. The grand jury meets on a regular basis to decide if crimes have been committed and whether to return an indictment charging a person with a crime. The grand jury process is confidential and if one appears before a grand jury, they cannot disclose what happened at the hearing. If they disclose what happened at the grand jury to others, they could be prosecuted for doing so. Below is an example of a grand jury subpoena to help you identify it and to also inform you of the possible penalties you could face if you do not properly respond to the subpoena.

AO110 (Rev. 12/89) Subpoena to Testify Before Grand Jury

UNITED STATES DISTRICT COURT

EASTERN   DISTRICT OF   TEXAS

TO: Custodian of Records   #
       Custodian of Records

**SUBPOENA TO TESTIFY
BEFORE GRAND JURY**

SUBPOENA FOR:
☐ PERSON   ☒ DOCUMENT(S) OR OBJECT(S)

YOU ARE HEREBY COMMANDED to appear and testify before the Grand Jury of the United States District Court at the place, date, and time specified below.

PLACE	COURTROOM
UNITED STATES COURTHOUSE	GRAND JURY ROOM.
7940 PRESTON ROAD	DATE AND TIME
PLANO, TEXAS 75024	2/12/2014 09:00

YOU ARE ALSO COMMANDED to bring with you the following document(s) or object(s):*
See attached

☐ *Please see additional information on reverse.*

This subpoena shall remain in effect until you are granted leave to depart by the court or by an officer acting on behalf of the court.

CLERK	DATE
David Whalen	12/20/2013
(By) Deputy Clerk	

This subpoena is issued on application of the United States of America

NAME, ADDRESS AND PHONE NUMBER OF ASSISTANT U.S. ATTORNEY

* If not applicable enter "none"

ATTACHMENT TO SUBPOENA

, Custodian of Records

You are hereby commanded to provide copies of all records for the period of **10/01/2010** to the present pertaining to transactions involving the following entities:

1.
   Owner/President:
   Address:

2.
   Owner/President:
   Address:

3.
   Member:
   Address:

Such records shall include, but are not limited to the following:

1. Records pertaining to any business transactions occurring with or on behalf of the above named entities (e.g., contracts, agreements, documents pertaining to the role of 67 Union Place, LLC in any transactions involving the above named entities, etc.);
2. Any and all contact information for the above named entities (e.g., name, address, telephone number, e-mail address, etc.);
3. Payment information for any transactions involving the above named entities (e.g. payment method, payment account number, wire transfer information, etc.);
4. Billing information for any transactions involving the above named entities (e.g. billing name, billing address, billing telephone number, invoices, receipts, wire transfer information, etc.);
5. Correspondence with individuals associated with the above named entities (e.g., e-mail correspondence, letters, and other memoranda);

Any questions regarding compliance with this subpoena should be directed to
          at   **Please deliver the requested items to**   Federal
Bureau of Investigation, One Justice Way, Dallas, Texas 75220.

Version 09/22/2019

INSTRUCTIONS FOR COMPLIANCE

In relation to the documents that you have been asked to produce, please follow the below instructions carefully when complying with the subpoena request.

INSTRUCTIONS FOR PRODUCTION OF RECORDS

I. General

    A.   Records existing as **Electronically Stored Information (ESI)** shall be produced in electronic form and shall include text data and image data held:

        1.   In your record retention systems; and/or

        2.   By your technology, data, or other service provider(s).

    B.   Records that do not exist as ESI may be produced in paper or other original format and may be converted to image or text data and provided as ESI, unless originals are required.

II. Text Data

    A.   Text data relating to transactions shall be produced within a data file:

        1.   Using a delimited ASCII text data format; or

        2.   Using software that can export to a commonly readable, non-proprietary file format without loss of data.

    B.   Text data files relating to transactions shall include field descriptions (e.g., account number, date/time, description, payee/payor, check number, item identifier, and amount).

III. Image Data

    A.   Image data shall be produced in graphic data files in a commonly readable, non-proprietary format with the highest image quality maintained.

    B.   Image data of items associated with transactions (e.g., checks and deposit slips) shall be:

        1.   Produced in individual graphic data files with any associated endorsements; and

        2.   Linked to corresponding text data by a unique identifier.

IV. Encryption/Authentication

    A.   ESI may be transmitted in an encrypted container. Decryption keys and/or passwords shall be produced separately at the time the data are produced.

    B.   Authentication, such as hash coding, may be set by agreement.

    C.   Affidavits or certificates of authenticity may be included as part of the electronic production.

Version 09/23/2010

V.   Cost Reimbursement

    A.   Costs that are reasonably necessary and have been directly incurred in searching for, reproducing, or transporting records may be reimbursable. See the *Right to Financial Privacy Act*, 12 U.S.C., Section 3415 and Federal Reserve Board *Regulation S*, 12 C.F.R., Part 219 (revised effective 1/1/2010).

Page 2 of 2

U.S. Department of Justice
United States Attorney
Eastern District of Texas

101 E. Park Boulevard, Suite 500   Telephone: (972) 509-1201
Plano, Texas 75074   Fax: (972) 509-1209
http://www.justice.gov/usao/txe/

December 20, 2013

Custodian of Records

Re: Grand Jury Subpoena #

Dear Custodian of Records:

Pursuant to an official criminal investigation of suspected federal offenses being conducted by a federal grand jury in the Eastern District of Texas, your institution has been called upon to furnish the documents and information described in the attached subpoena.

As a recipient of a grand jury subpoena for financial institution records, you should be aware that civil and criminal penalties now exist for making certain disclosures regarding this subpoena. The prohibited notifications and applicable penalties are stated in sections 943 and 962 of the Financial Institutions Reform, Recovery and Enforcement Act of 1989 (12 U.S.C. § 3420(b) and 18 U.S.C. § 1519(b)), respectively.

The criminal penalties include fines and a maximum prison term of five years if an employee, officer, director, partner, agent or attorney of a financial institution notifies, directly or indirectly, any person regarding the existence or contents of this subpoena with the intent to obstruct a judicial proceeding. In addition, if there is no showing of an intent to obstruct a judicial proceeding, fines and a maximum prison term of one year may be imposed if the notification is made, directly or indirectly, to a customer of the financial institution whose records are sought by the subpoena or to any other person named in the subpoena. Civil money penalties may also be imposed.

Therefore, you are not to disclose the existence of this subpoena or the fact of your compliance with it. If you have any questions, or if you are considering a disclosure, please contact the undersigned federal prosecutor.

Your cooperation in this matter is appreciated.

ATTACHMENT

Unless explicitly indicated otherwise, the following words or phrases are used herein as follows:

(1) "Document" or "records" refers to all written or graphic matter, however produced or reproduced, or to any other tangible permanent record, and, without limitation, including, among other things, all letters, correspondence, records, memoranda, minutes, notes, summaries, telephone records, books, schedules, reports, studies, appraisals, analyses, lists, interviews, books of account, telegrams, notes and minutes of meetings, interoffice communications, results of investigations, working papers, computer data, financial instruments including money orders, cashier checks and personal checks, papers similar to any of the foregoing and other writings of every kind of description (whether or not actually used, and including drafts of all documents), and including not only originals of such documents but all photostatic or microfilmed copies in whatever form, and all sound records or electronic data compilations in whatever form.

(2) A document "relating or incident to" a given subject matter means any document or communication that constitutes, contains, embodies, comprises, reflects, identifies, describes, analyzes, or is in any way pertinent to that subject, including, without limitation, documents concerning the presentation of other documents.

(3) A document within your "possession and control" includes not only those in your direct possession, but also those documents in the possession of another person which you have the right to claim or possess.

(4) "Document(s)" also includes all items which are subject to a claim of privilege. If any such documents are responsive to the subpoena, each page of the "privileged" document will be numbered consecutively, and placed in a sealed envelope to be held by the custodian until directed otherwise by the Court. The custodian will then provide the Grand Jury with a log which states the following with respect to each document withheld: 1) the date of the document; 2) author; 3) primary addresses; 4) secondary addresses; 5) type of document; 6) client; 7) attorney; 8) subject matter of document; 9) purpose of the document; and 10) whether the document is work product or attorney-client privilege.

(5) "Entity" [or "company"] means any and all of the following: [entity or company names and any variations thereof], and any and all predecessors, successors, parent organizations, subsidiaries, affiliates, branches, divisions, units or offices of such entity [or company].

Pursuant to the enclosed grand jury subpoena, you are required to produce original documents (unless otherwise specified) at the time and place indicated on the subpoena. Alternatively, you may comply with this subpoena by delivering the requested documents to _____, FBI, One Justice Way, Dallas, Texas 75220. The records should be accompanied by an affidavit, signed by the records custodian, stating that the records produced represent all business records in your care, custody and control which comply with the subpoena. If documents have been withheld from production, the affidavit should describe the withheld documents in detail and reflect a detailed basis for withholding the documents.

If production will not be complete by the return date, you will need to obtain a continuance from me. Additionally, you should send a letter to _____ before the stated return date identifying the documents which have not yet been produced and specifying the reasons for the delay. Once the subpoenaed records are ready to be produced, please mail documents to _____, and **not to me.**

If you have any questions concerning the subpoena or the documents and records requested, please contact me.

Sincerely,

JOHN M. BALES
United States Attorney
Eastern District of Texas

Assistant United States Attorney

Attachments

3

YOU ARE PRESENTED WITH A SEARCH WARRANT

I F YOU OR your business is presented with a search warrant to seize any type of business documents or computers at home or office, it is an obvious signal that you are under a criminal investigation.

In order for a search warrant to be issued and signed by a federal judge, a federal law enforcement officer has to swear to an affidavit *to all the facts he/she is relying on to* establish probable cause that a crime has been committed and evidence of the crime is located in the person's home, business, automobile, computer, storage shed, etc. *and thus must be seized as proof.* So, if a search warrant has been issued, the agents believe you have committed a crime at that point and a federal judge has agreed with that belief. You cannot refuse the law enforcement access to your home or business, but you can contact an attorney as quickly as possible to ensure that the agents do not behave outside the scope of the search warrant, such as seizing items that are not covered by the warrant or searching places that they are not authorized to search. On the next page, you will see a search warrant for your review.

AO 93 (Rev. 11/13) Search and Seizure Warrant

UNITED STATES DISTRICT COURT
for the
EASTERN DISTRICT OF TEXAS

In the Matter of the Search of *(Briefly describe the property to be searched or identify the person by name and address)* Premisis at	)))))) Case No.

SEARCH AND SEIZURE WARRANT

To: Any authorized law enforcement officer

     An application by a federal law enforcement officer or an attorney for the government requests the search of the following person or property located in the   Eastern   District of   Texas
(Identify the person or describe the property to be searched and give its location):

Premises at   located in the Eastern District of Texas, see attachment A, which is attached herto and incorporated herein by refernce.

     I find that the affidavit(s), or any recorded testimony, establish probable cause to search and seize the person or property described above, and that such search will reveal *(identify the person or describe the property to be seized):*
SEE ATTACHMENT B, WHICH IS ATTACHED HERETO AND INCORPORATED HEREIN BY REFERENCE.

     YOU ARE COMMANDED to execute this warrant on or before   5-23-14   *(not to exceed 14 days)*
☑ in the daytime 6:00 a.m. to 10:00 p.m.   ☐ at any time in the day or night because good cause has been established.

     Unless delayed notice is authorized below, you must give a copy of the warrant and a receipt for the property taken to the person from whom, or from whose premises, the property was taken, or leave the copy and receipt at the place where the property was taken.

     The officer executing this warrant, or an officer present during the execution of the warrant, must prepare an inventory as required by law and promptly return this warrant and inventory to   Judge Don D. Bush
                                                                        (United States Magistrate Judge)

     ☐ Pursuant to 18 U.S.C. § 3103a(b), I find that immediate notification may have an adverse result listed in 18 U.S.C. § 2705 (except for delay of trial), and authorize the officer executing this warrant to delay notice to the person who, or whose property, will be searched or seized *(check the appropriate box)*
     ☐ for _____ days *(not to exceed 30)*   ☐ until, the facts justifying, the later specific date of _____ .

Date and time issued: 05/09/2014 10:00 am	*Judge's signature*
City and state: Plano, TX	Don. D. Bush, U. S. Magistrate Judge *Printed name and title*

4

RECEIPT OF A TARGET LETTER

THE USE OF target letters is one thing that is fairly unique to federal white collar criminal investigations. This is a letter that is sent by the prosecuting attorney to a person or a business informing them that there is an open investigation and that the person or business is/are the subject or target of that investigation. The letter will generally let the person know the purpose of the investigation and what rights and responsibilities a person has. It will also request that they contact the prosecuting attorney within so many days to discuss the matter. If you receive this kind of letter, it is imperative that you contact an experienced criminal defense attorney immediately. An experienced criminal defense attorney can negotiate with the Assistant United States Attorney so you are only a witness and not a defendant. By intervening early, an experienced criminal defense attorney can convince a prosecutor to close the investigation and to not bring forth charges. In the unfortunate event that you have committed a crime, your attorney can negotiate with the prosecuting attorney to limit your exposure by reducing the charges or by cooperating in the investigation. It is imperative that you do not hesitate to contact an attorney upon receipt of this type of letter. Any delay on your part could cause you to miss an opportunity for your attorney to create a favorable outcome. Please turn the page to view a sample target letter.

U.S. Department of Justice

United States Attorney
Northern District of Texas

1100 Commerce Street, Third Floor	*Main: 214.659.8600*
Dallas, Texas 75242-1699	*Fax: 214.659.8812*

January 8, 2015

VIA HAND DELIVERY

Re: Target Letter

Dear   :

This letter is to advise that you are the target of a federal grand jury investigation concerning possible violations of federal law.

This particular investigation concerns allegations of that you were involved in a conspiracy involving identity theft and bank fraud. Having reviewed the circumstances involved in this case, I believe it is appropriate to formally charge you with Conspiracy to Commit Bank Fraud, a violation of 18 U.S.C. § 1349, among other charges.

However, I am prepared to consider negotiating a plea agreement with you as an alternative to presenting this case to the Grand Jury for indictment. Should you be interested in negotiating a plea agreement, please notify   at the number below and we will arrange a time to meet and discuss this matter with you and your attorney.

If you do not want to negotiate a plea, you are invited to appear before a grand jury in the Northern District of Texas to testify about matters related to the above-referenced conduct. Understand that your decision to testify will be completely voluntary and that your testimony could be used against you if any criminal charges are returned.

Since I have not been contacted or advised otherwise, I presume you do not currently have an attorney in connection with these possible charges. If you are financially unable to hire an attorney to assist you, you should contact the Court and fill out the appropriate financial affidavit to obtain a court-appointed attorney. You can contact   at   to obtain this financial affidavit.

In order for the Court to appoint you an attorney at government expense, the judge will have to review your financial situation and determine if you qualify. If you do qualify, an attorney will be appointed to assist you, and you will be contacted by the Federal Public Defender's Office or another defense attorney appointed by the Court.

Be advised, if   or I do not hear from you or your attorney by Friday, January 30, 2015, I will conclude that a plea agreement is not an alternative you want to consider, and this office will proceed accordingly with your prosecution.

If you have any questions, please contact   at

Sincerely,

JOHN R. PARKER
ACTING UNITED STATES ATTORNEY

_____

Assistant United States Attorney

PART TWO
WHAT TO DO

5

Don't panic! Call an attorney

I F YOU WERE contacted by law enforcement in person, received a target letter, were served with a subpoena or search warrant, don't panic...call an
attorney! That is often easier said than done, especially if this is your first en-
counter with law enforcement and it involves a federal agent; in order to protect
yourself, it is a must. I have observed people panic and make matters worse by
shredding documents or telling potential witnesses what to say or do. These
behaviors will turn a small problem into a major problem very quickly and may
hinder your attorney's ability to facilitate a favorable outcome.

The best thing to do is call an experienced criminal defense attorney to
ensure that your rights are safeguarded at all times. He or she will provide
guidance and help you understand what is happening by removing a great deal
of uncertainty and giving you peace of mind that everything will be okay in
the end. You should look for an experienced criminal defense attorney who has
extensive federal criminal defense experience. Additionally, look for a Board
Certified Criminal Defense Attorney who has dedicated the majority of their
law practice to helping people accused of crimes.

6

DO NOT ANSWER QUESTIONS

MANY PEOPLE UNDER investigation talk to law enforcement before they understand how the information will be used. Sometimes they yield because they have been threatened with arrest. Do not be fooled and give them details that could later potentially compromise you. As a society, we have been conditioned to cooperate with law enforcement, but it is okay and within your **RIGHTS** to tell a federal agent that you want to speak to an attorney before answering his/her questions.

Some agents will attempt to intimidate you by saying things like, "We can have this conversation here or downtown." Comments like this signal an unreasonable and aggressive attitude. Even if the investigator is polite, do not be fooled--it is their job to collect information and evidence, not help you. It is the job of your lawyer to help you navigate the legal system and to advocate on your behalf.

To illustrate the point, I have had several clients talk to law enforcement because they felt they had nothing to hide or thought if they just explained their side of the story it would make the situation disappear. Unfortunately, for these clients, the outcome was that their statements ended up strengthening the case against them. Law enforcement agents are allowed to lie to you in order to get you to confess. If you ask an agent, "Should I get a lawyer", most will try and talk you out of it. I had a client ask that very same question and was told, "Why do you need a lawyer if you have nothing to hide?" The client fell for this and talked to the agents. A week later, that client received a target letter, which possibly could have been avoided if he had contacted an experienced criminal defense attorney prior to speaking to the agent.

If a federal agent gives you a Miranda warning saying, "You have the right to remain silent", know that you are definitely the subject of a criminal investigation. Say nothing further without an attorney present. If you request an attorney, all questioning is supposed to end immediately. If they continue to attempt to question you, just say, "I want my attorney." In my experience, I have come to believe that you can never win by giving statements to police without the aid of an attorney. The predicament seems to be that if you do not answer their questions, they are going to think you have something to hide; but if you do give a statement and you do not admit you're guilty then they will say that you are lying. As the saying goes, "You're damned if you do and damned if you don't." Protect yourself and do not answer any questions. Additionally, by giving a statement without the full knowledge of what is actually taking place will limit your defense later. Once you give that statement, it is on permanent record. Any attempt to change statements at a later date will cause you to lose credibility. My experience also has been that by giving a statement early, it gives the government ample time to find what you said to be erroneous as well as using it to anticipate your defense. Err on the side of caution by keeping your mouth shut!

7

IF YOU DO ANSWER QUESTIONS, TELL THE TRUTH

I F YOU DISREGARD the sound legal advice in Chapter Six and choose instead to talk to law enforcement, I encourage you to tell the truth. All it takes is just one lie to make you look guilty. A single lie will solidify the government's belief that you are guilty and thus makes it easier for them to convince a jury that you are guilty. The general belief is that only guilty people lie to the police. Additionally, giving false information or lying to a federal agent is a crime. You can face up to five years in federal prison for lying to a federal agent. It is natural to want to defend yourself by explaining what happened, but remember, investigators are only there to seek evidence, not to see your point of view. It is the prosecutor, not the investigator, who makes the decision regarding prosecution. Save any explanations for your attorney who can speak with the prosecutor on your behalf.

8

DO NOT CONSENT TO ANY SEARCH OF YOUR HOME OR BUSINESS WITHOUT A WARRANT

I F ANY FEDERAL agent asks you if they can search your home or business, or asks you to surrender anything, make sure they have a legal right to request the items. Federal law enforcement agents cannot search your home, office, vehicle, phone, or computer without a search warrant, unless you consent. If you consent to a search, you cannot complain later that they did not have a warrant. If law enforcement agent asks to search your home, office, phone, or computer, ask if they have a warrant. If they do not have a warrant, tell them **NO**!

Once I had a client who turned over his computer to the FBI simply because they asked. The FBI then searched that computer and found a mountain of incriminating evidence, which led to charges filed, and ultimately, a prison sentence. Why would a federal law enforcement agent request a consensual search? The most likely reason is that he/she doesn't have enough evidence to convince a judge to issue a search warrant. Do not consent to any type of search without first consulting an attorney. If they do present you with a warrant, consult an attorney and do not interfere with the agent's ability to execute the warrant.

9

DO NOT SURRENDER ANY DOCUMENTS
WITHOUT A SUBPOENA

I F A FEDERAL law enforcement agent requests documents from you, do not produce anything unless presented with a subpoena or if they have a warrant to seize the documents. Generally, you are under no legal obligation to surrender documents unless they are properly subpoenaed.

If you are served with the subpoena, you are legally obligated to comply with the subpoena. **DO NOT IGNORE** the subpoena. If you fail to comply with a subpoena in any way, you could be charged with obstruction of justice and could face time in federal prison. Hire an attorney to help you. Your attorney will contact the U.S. Attorney's office or agent to determine what they need, and will then advise you on how to comply to the best of your ability.

If you are ever served with a subpoena, do not destroy any requested documents. The destruction of documents can also lead to a possible obstruction of justice charge. Additionally, you cannot tell anyone other than your attorney that you have been served with the subpoena. If you do, you can be subject to criminal penalties for the disclosure. So, if you are served with a subpoena, hire an attorney to help you comply with the subpoena and prevent you from potentially violating the law.

Conclusion

I HOPE THE ABOVE information has been helpful in recognizing the signs that you may be under investigation for a federal with collar crime and some tips on what do if you are. I also hope that this book will help readers to gain a better understanding of the process of criminal investigation and their rights if they are a possible subject of one. I hope that you never have to utilize this book, but in the event you do, or know someone who should, the information contained in this book should give you the confidence to handle the situation in a way that protects you and your rights.

Conclusion